My name is ______________________________.

Draw a picture of your favourite funny character from a story.

____

(character name)

____

(story title)

Handwriting: anticlockwise letter; body letter (a).
Grammar: nouns; saying verbs (agree, arguing, ask); how adverb (angrily); statement.
Punctuation: full stop; capital letter to start a sentence.

Spelling and vocabulary: act, add, agree, angrily, ant, ape, apple, are, arguing, asked, away, day, today.
Literary elements: rhyme (away/day); Welsh proverb (Eat an apple on going to bed and you'll keep the doctor from earning his bread.

Trace and finish the pattern.

Write the date.

Write.

a A

Use a to finish these words. Trace the words.

pe go w y tod y d y

Trace then write.

An apple a day keeps

the doctor away.

Self-assessment

How many a's did you write on this page?

Circle your best a.

Handwriting: anticlockwise letter; body letter (c).
Grammar: nouns; action verbs (cutting, crept); saying verbs (croaked, called); how adverb (cleverly); irregular verb (creep/crept); question; question word (What?); proper nouns (Mama, Baby, Pop).
Punctuation: question mark; capital letter to start a sentence.
Spelling and vocabulary: word families (cut, cutting, cuts; creep, creeping, creeps, crept); apostrophe for contraction (where's); called, camel, cleverly, corn, creep, crept, croaked, cutting, popcorn.
Literary elements: riddle; joke; word play; onomatopoeia (croak).

Trace and finish the pattern.

Write the date.

Use c to finish these words. Trace the words.

ut uts utting

reep reeps rept reeping

Trace then write.

What did Baby corn say

to Mama corn? Where's

Pop corn?

Self-assessment

Draw a frame around your best c and your best C on each page.

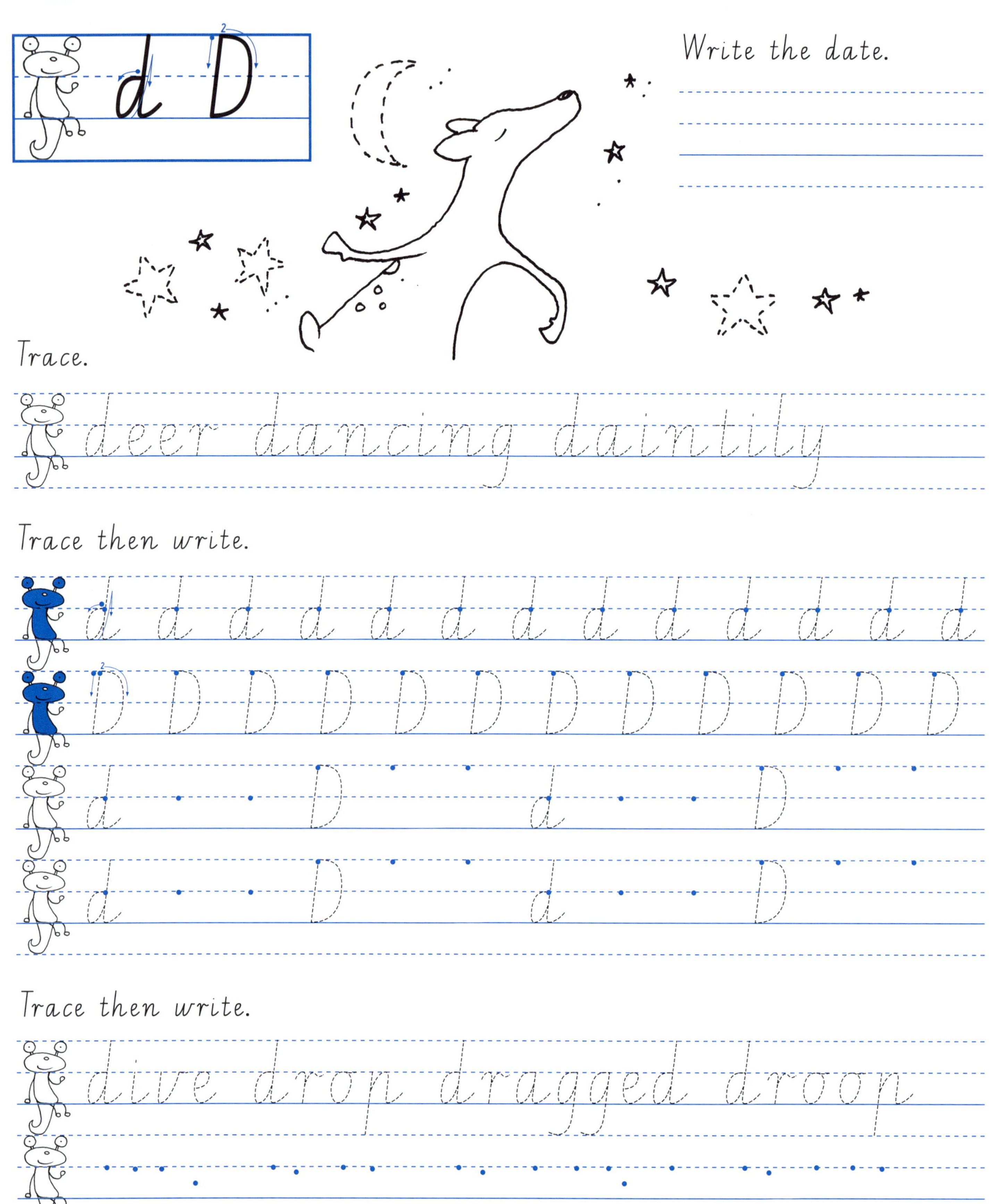

Handwriting: anticlockwise letter; head and body letter (ascender) (d).
Grammar: noun; action verbs (dive, drop, drag, droop); how adverb (daintily); question; question word (When?).
Punctuation: full stop; question mark; capital letter to start a sentence.
Spelling and vocabulary: word families (dance, danced, dancing, dances); daintily, dancing, deer, dinosaur, dive, dragged, droop, drop; when to double final consonant to add suffix -ed (drag, dragged).
Literary elements: riddle; joke; word play (dinosaur/sore).

Trace and finish the pattern.

eelee

Write the date.

Find and trace d.

d f h d t k m d p a h f d

Use d to finish these words. Trace the words.

ance ances anced

Trace then write.

When do dinosaurs need

bandages? When they get

dino-sores.

Self-assessment

Draw a tick above every d on this page.

Circle your best d.

Handwriting: anticlockwise letter; body and tail letter (descender) (g).
Grammar: nouns; verbs; how adverb (gladly); past tense (-ed); question; question word (Why?).
Punctuation: full stop; question mark; capital letter to start a sentence.

Spelling and vocabulary: word families (gave, give, gives, giving); fight, fright, knight, sight, gladly, gobbled, gorilla, groaned, guzzled; silent k (knight); suffixes -ly, -ing, -ed (gladly, giving, groaned).
Literary elements: riddle; joke; word play; homophones (night/knight).

Trace and finish the pattern.

Write the date.

Find and trace g.

g b d q d g h b m q g

Use g to finish these words. Trace the words.

ive ives ave iving

Trace then write.

Why do dragons sleep

all day? So they can go

fight knights.

Self-assessment

Draw a frame around your best g on each page.

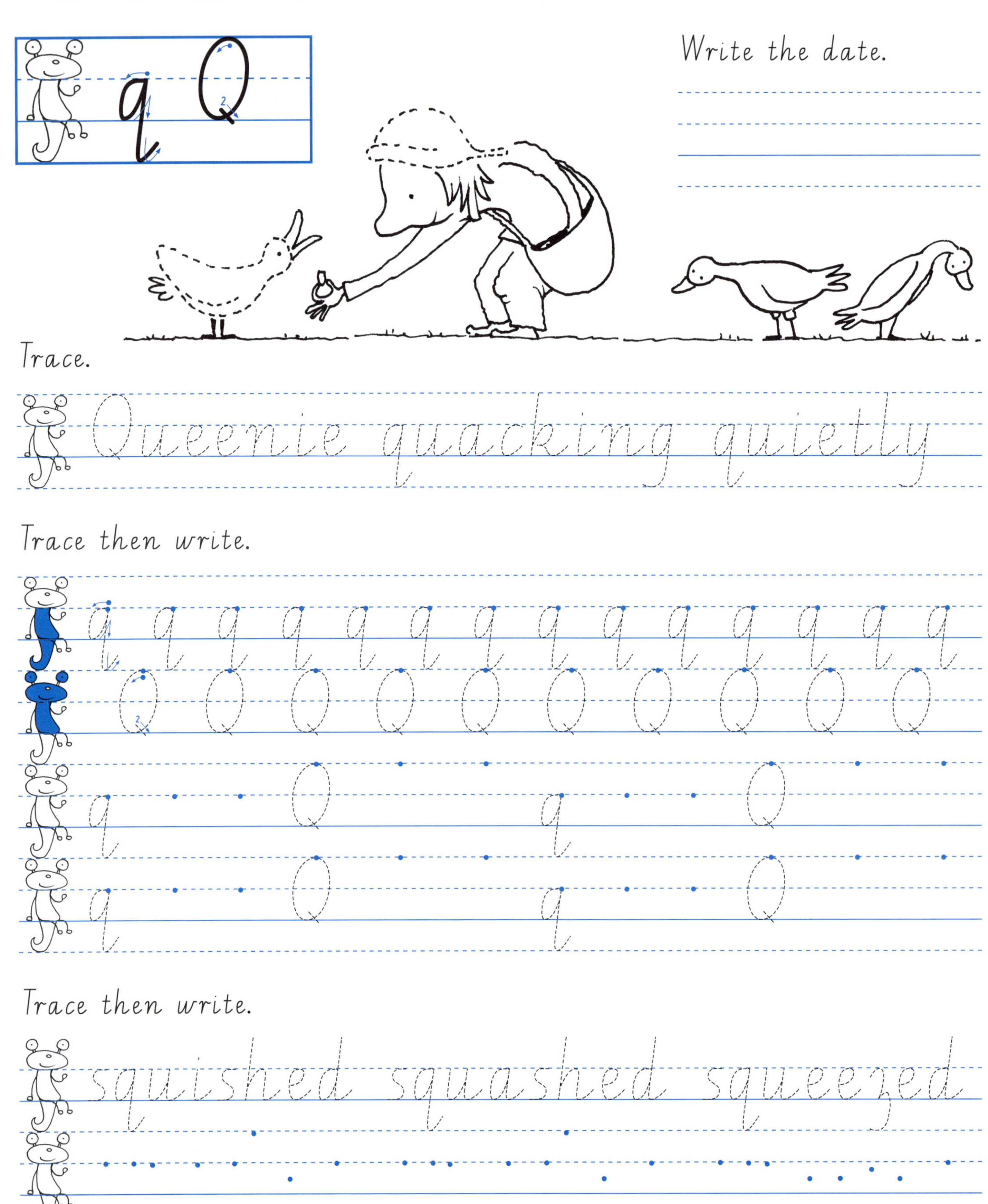

Handwriting: anticlockwise letter; body and tail letter (descender) (q).
Grammar: proper noun (Queenie); action verbs (squished, squashed, squeezed); saying verb (quacking); how adverb (quietly); question; question word (What?).
Punctuation: full stop; question mark; capital letter to start a sentence.

Spelling and vocabulary: word families (quack, quacked, quacking, quacks); apostrophe for contraction (I've); qu and squ (quacking, quietly, quilt, squashed, squeezed, squished); suffixes -ing, -ily, -ed (quacking, quietly, squished).
Literary elements: riddle; joke; word play (quilt/covered).

Trace and finish the pattern.

elel

Write the date.

Find and trace the body and tail letters.

q v g y w q a g v w a

Use q to finish these words. Trace the words.

uack uacks uacked

Trace then write.

What did the quilt say

to the bed? I've got you

covered.

Self-assessment

Circle your best q.

Underline the q's you could improve.

Handwriting: anticlockwise letter; body letter (e).
Grammar: nouns; action verbs (sleep, eating); saying verb (cheep); how adverb (eagerly); statement.
Punctuation: full stop; capital letter to start a sentence.

Spelling and vocabulary: word families (ate, eat, eating, eats); 'ee' (cheep, peep, sleep, sneeze); 'ph' (elephant, phone, photo); rhyme (healthy/wealthy, wise/rise, peep/cheep/sleep).
Literary elements: moral; proverb (published 1735, attributed to Benjamin Franklin); onomatopoeia (cheep).

Trace and finish the pattern.

Write the date.

Use e to finish these words. Trace the words.

at ats ating at

Trace then write.

Early to bed and early

to rise, makes you healthy,

wealthy and wise.

Self-assessment

Draw triangles around three e's with the best shape.

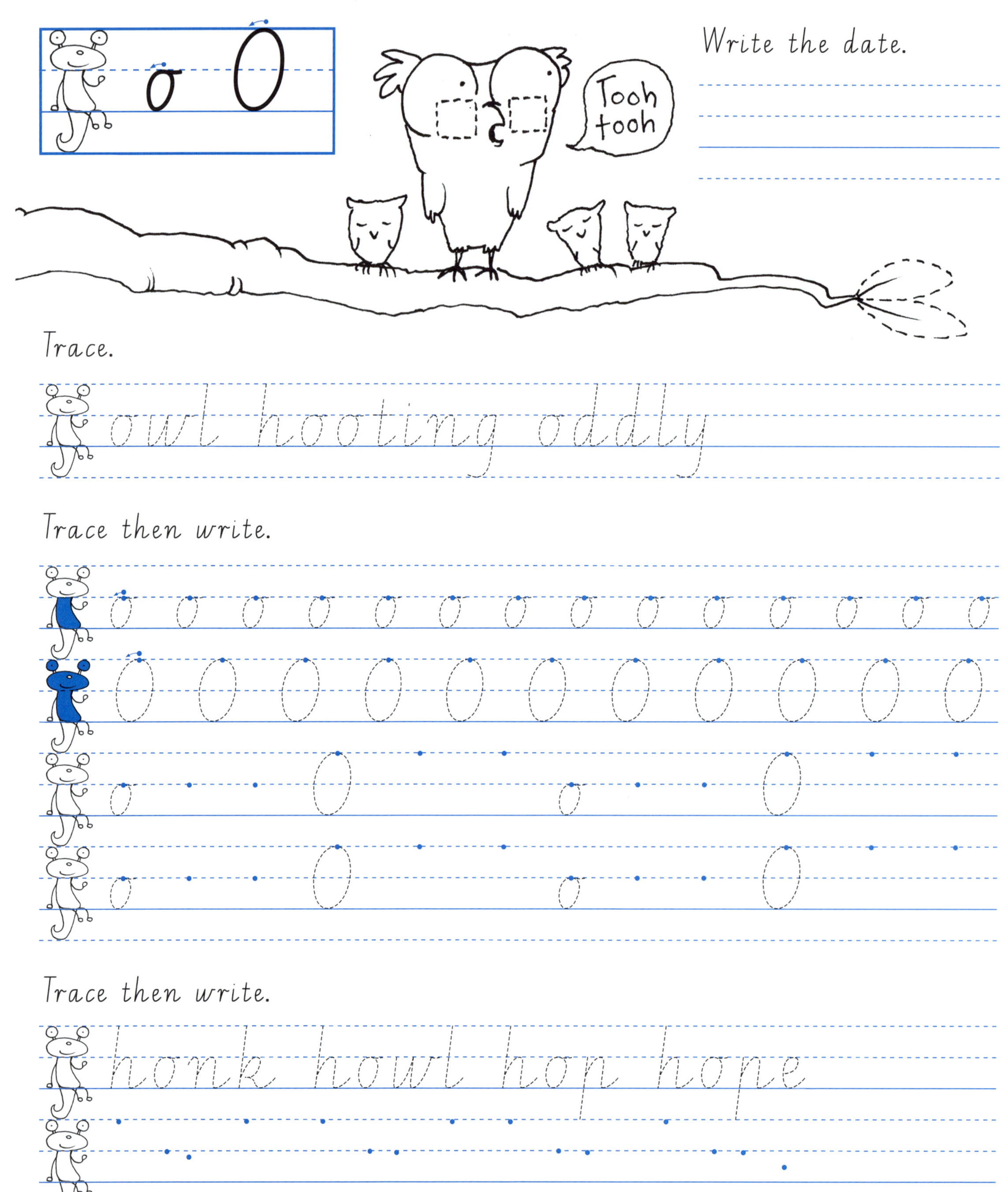

Handwriting: anticlockwise letter; body letter (o).
Grammar: nouns; gender nouns (cow/bull); saying verbs (hoot, howl, honk); how adverb (oddly); question; question word (What?); irregular verb (does/do).
Punctuation: full stop; question mark; capital letter to start a sentence.

Spelling and vocabulary: 'ow' (cow, howl, owl); 'oo' (hoot, hooted, hooting, hoots, moo); word families (hop, hopped, hopping, hops); honk, hope, oddly.
Literary elements: riddle; joke; word play (moo-vies); onomatopoeia (hoot, howl, honk).

Trace and finish the pattern.

Write the date.

Use o to finish these words. Trace the words.

h o o t h o o ts h o o ted h o o ting

h o p h o ps h o pped h o pping

Trace then write.

What does the cow like to do on her day off? Go to the moo-vies.

Self-assessment

Circle the o on each page that has the best shape.

Handwriting: anticlockwise letter; head, body and tail letter (ascender and descender) (f).
Grammar: nouns; action verbs (fly, fling, floating); how adverb (freely); question; question word (What?); proper nouns (Friday, Frank).
Punctuation: question mark; capital letter to start a sentence.
Spelling and vocabulary: 'ch' digraph (chases); when to double final consonant to add -ed (flopped, flapped, stopped, hopped); 'fl' blend (fling, floating, flopped); 'sh' digraph (fish); word families (float, floated, floating, floats).
Literary elements: riddle; joke; word play.

Trace and finish the pattern.

Write the date.

Write.

f F

Use f or F to finish these words. Trace the words.

riday inger rank irst

loat loats loated

Trace then write.

What kind of fish chases

a mouse? A catfish.

Self-assessment

Highlight or underline ALL the fs on this page.

Circle your best f.

Write the date.

Trace.

snake stopping suddenly

Trace then write.

Trace then write.

swing sway sob say stop

Handwriting: anticlockwise letter; body letter (s).
Grammar: noun; action verbs (stopping, swing, sway); saying verbs (sob, say); how adverb (suddenly); statement.
Punctuation: full stop; capital letter to start a sentence.

Spelling and vocabulary: when to double final consonant to add -ing (stopping); blends with s: sn (snake), st (stop, sticks, stones), sw (sway, swing); word families (stop, stopped, stopping, stops); suffix -ly, (suddenly).
Literary elements: children's rhyme (dated to 1862).

Trace and finish the pattern.

Write the date.

Use s to finish these words. Trace the words.

top top topped topping

Trace then write.

Sticks and stones may

break my bones but words

will never hurt me.

Self-assessment

Draw a square around the word that shows your best handwriting.

m M

Write the date.

Trace.

meerkats munching merrily

Trace then write.

m m m m m m m m m

M M M M M M M M M

m M m M

m M m M

Trace then write.

missed mind moped move

Handwriting: clockwise letter; body letter (m).
Grammar: plural noun (meerkats); proper nouns (Mars, Martian); verbs; how adverb (merrily); adjectives (soft, white); question; question word (What's?).
Punctuation: question mark; capital letter to start a sentence.
Spelling and vocabulary: apostrophe for contraction (what's); meerkat, mind, missed, move; suffixes -ing, -ly, -ed (merrily, moped); word families (munch, munched, munches, munching).
Literary elements: riddle; joke; word play (marshmallow/Martian-mallow).

Trace and finish the pattern.

Write the date.

Use m to finish these words. Trace the words.

unch unches unched

Trace then write.

What's soft and white

and lives on Mars?

A Martian-mallow.

Self-assessment

Are your m's all the same size?

Handwriting: clockwise letter; body letter (n).
Grammar: nouns; feeling verb (needed); thinking verb (noticed); how adverb (noisily); statement.
Punctuation: full stop; capital letter to start a sentence; possessive apostrophe (sailor's).

Spelling and vocabulary: night, delight, morning, needed, neigh, nibbling, nod, noisily, noticed, numbat, pink, sailor, warning; suffixes -ily, -ing (noisily, warning, nibbling); word families (nibble, nibbled, nibbles).
Literary elements: ancient rhyme (over 2000 years old) for weather forecasting; onomatopoeia (neigh); rhyme (night/delight, warning/morning).

Trace and finish the pattern.

Write the date.

Use n to finish these words. Trace the words.

·ibble ·ibbles ·ibbled

Trace then write.

Pink in the morning a

sailor's warning. Pink in

the night, a sailor's delight.

Self-assessment

How many n's did you write on this page?

Draw a square around an n you could improve.

Handwriting: clockwise letter; body letter (r).
Grammar: nouns; action verbs (riding, rub, roll, rush, ripped); how adverb (rapidly); joining word (because); question; question word (Why?).
Punctuation: question mark; capital letter to start a sentence; upper case for sounds (aRRR); exclamation mark.

Spelling and vocabulary: word families (ride, rides, riding, rode); pirate, press, rat, rapidly, red, rest, riding, ripped, rock, roll, room, rub, rug, rush.
Literary elements: riddle; joke; word play; onomatopoeia (aRRR); rhyme (are/aRRR).

Trace and finish the pattern.

Write the date.

Write.

r R

Use r to finish these words. Trace the words.

ug oom ed p ess est

ide ides iding ode

Trace then write.

Why are pirates called

pirates? Because they aRRR!

Self-assessment

How many R's are on these two pages?

Circle your best capital R.

Handwriting: clockwise letter; body letter (x).
Grammar: nouns; action verbs (fix, flex, mix, relaxing); how adverb (flexibly); statement.
Punctuation: full stop; capital letter to start a sentence.
Spelling and vocabulary: word families (relax, relaxed, relaxes, relaxing); fax, fix, flex, flexibly, mix; 'oa' vowel digraph (coax, float, boat, groan, moan); pixie, relaxing, stubborn, text.
Literary elements: Aesop fable 'The reed and the olive tree', moral: It is better to be flexible than stubborn.

Trace and finish the pattern.

Write the date.

Write.

x X

Use x to finish these words. Trace the words.

bo fo gala y inde o

rela rela es rela ed

Trace then write.

It is better to be flexible

than stubborn.

Self-assessment

Tick your five best x's.

Draw a square around an X you could improve.

Handwriting: clockwise letter; body and tail letter (descender) (z).
Grammar: nouns; verbs; how adverb (zappily); question; question word (How?).
Punctuation: question mark; capital letter to start a sentence.

Spelling and vocabulary: drizzle, fizzed, grizzle; 'oo' vowel digraph (school); whiz, zappily, zonkey; rhyme (grizzle/drizzle); word families (zoom, zoomed, zooming, zooms).
Literary elements: portmanteau word (zonkey = zebra+donkey); riddle; joke; word play (buzz = bus); onomatopoeia (grizzle, fizzed).

Trace and finish the pattern.

Write the date.

Write.

z Z

Write the matching capital letters.

f m z x n r s

Use z to finish these words. Trace the words.

oom ooms oomed

Trace then write.

How does a bee get to school? In a buzz.

Self-assessment

Draw a square around the word that is your best handwriting on each page.

Handwriting: clockwise letter; head and body letter (ascender) (h).
Grammar: noun; verbs; how adverb (happily); question; question word (Why?).
Punctuation: full stop; question mark; capital letter to start a sentence.

Spelling and vocabulary: apostrophe for contraction (aren't); when to double final consonant to add suffix -ing or -ed (hopping, hugged, spotted); had, happily, help, hide, hippo, hit; 'e' to make long vowel sound (hide, hope); word families (hop, hopped, hopping, hops).
Literary elements: riddle; word play (spotted).

Trace and finish the pattern.

Write the date.

Use h to finish these words. Trace the words.

op ops opped opping

Trace then write.

Why aren't leopards any good at hide-and-seek?

They are always spotted.

Self-assessment

Draw a star around your best h and your best H on these two pages.

Handwriting: clockwise letter; head and body letter (ascender) (k).
Grammar: nouns; action verbs (kneel, kick, kissing); how adverb (kindly); statement.
Punctuation: full stop; capital letter to start a sentence.
Spelling and vocabulary: 'ck' consonant digraph (kick, knock, pocket, pluck); kangaroo, kindly; silent 'k' (kneel, knock); change y to i to add -ed (carried); word families (kiss, kissed, kisses, kissing).
Literary elements: simile (like a garden); Chinese proverb.

Trace and finish the pattern.

Write the date.

Write.

k K

Trace the letters that start like k.

l b o u y b a x h

Use k to finish these words. Trace the words.

iss isses issed issing

Trace then write.

A book is like a garden

carried in the pocket.

Self-assessment

How many k's did you write on this page?

Tick your best k.

Write the date.

Trace.

peacock prancing proudly

Trace then write.

p p p p p p p p p p p p

P P P P P P P P P P P P

Trace then write.

pout push poked peep pop

Handwriting: clockwise letter; body and tail letter (descender) (p).
Grammar: nouns; action verbs (push, poked, prancing); how adverb (proudly); statement; command starting with a verb (Be).
Punctuation: full stop; capital letter to start a sentence.
Spelling and vocabulary: word families (prance, pranced, prances, prancing; pop, popped, popping, pops); apostrophe for contraction (you've); male and female words (peacock/peahen); peep, poked, pop, pout, proudly; soft 'c' (prancing, dancing, fancy, ice).
Literary elements: moral (a bird in the hand is worth two in the bush, from various origins including Aesop's fable 'The Hawk and the Nightingale').

Trace and finish the pattern.

Write the date.

Write.

p P

Write the matching capital letters.

b k h m r n

Use p to finish these words. Trace the words.

rance rances ranced

o os o ed o ing

Trace then write.

Be happy with what

you've got.

Self-assessment

Circle the neatest p.

Underline the p's you could improve.

Handwriting: i family letter; body letter (i).
Grammar: nouns; action verbs (itching, slipping, lifting, sliding); how adverb (impolitely); statement.
Punctuation: full stop; capital letter to start a sentence.

Spelling and vocabulary: 'tch' trigraph (ditch, itch, switch, twitch); drop 'e' to add -ing (hiding, riding, sliding); 'nk' blend (drink, link, pink, stink); prefix im- (immature, impolite, impossible); word families (slid, slide, sliding; itch, itched, itches, itching); rhyme (drink/link/pink/stink, later/alligator, while/crocodile).
Literary elements: colloquialism/sayings and expressions.

Trace and finish the pattern.

Write the date.

Write.

i

Use i to finish these words. Trace the words.

nk dr nk p nk st nk l nk

tch tches tched tch ng

Trace then write.

See you later alligator.

In a while crocodile.

Self-assessment

Are your letters sloping evenly?

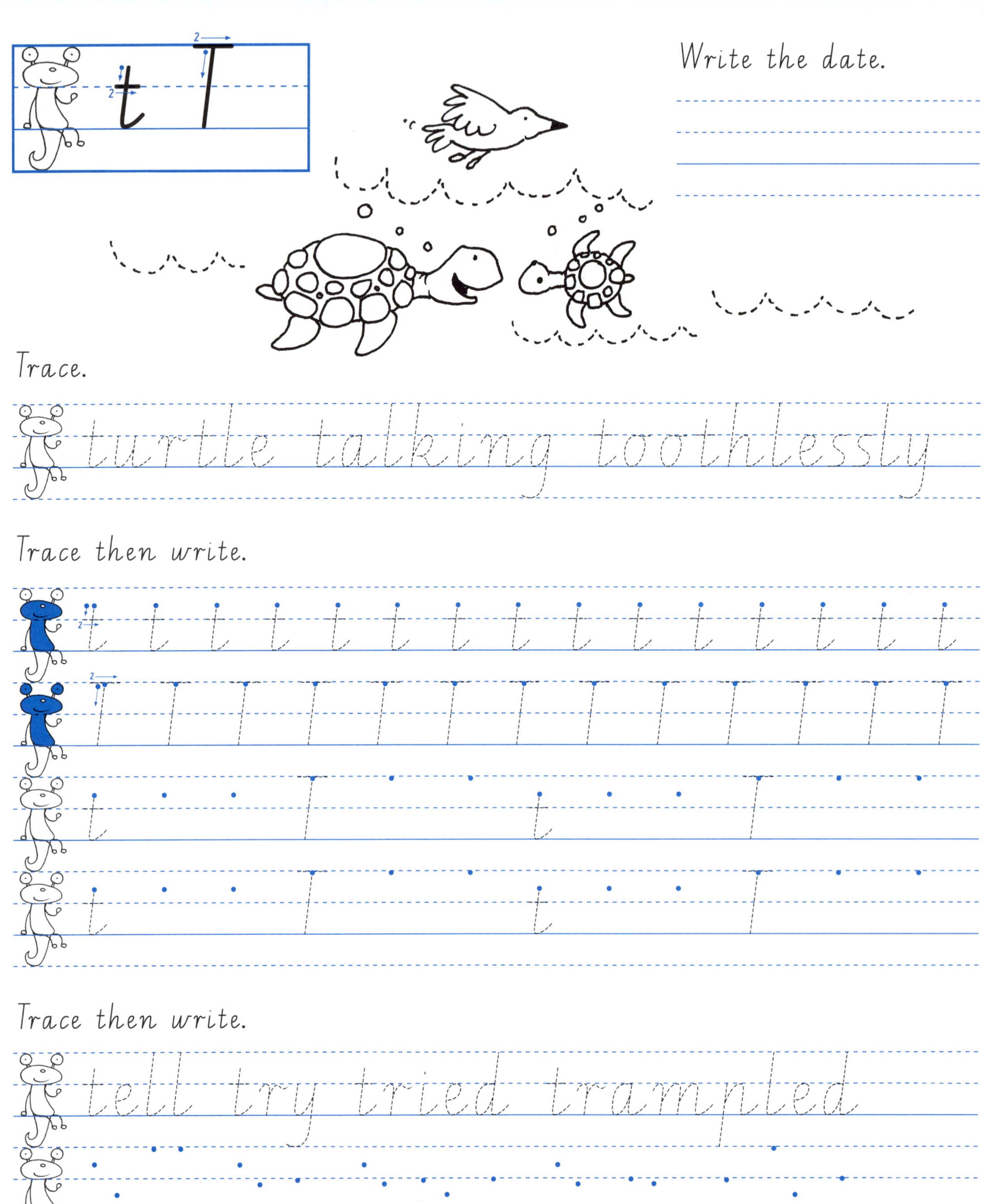

Handwriting: i family letter; head and body letter (ascender) (t).
Grammar: nouns; saying verbs (tell, talking); how adverb (toothlessly); question; question word (What?).
Punctuation: question mark; capital letter to start a sentence.

Spelling and vocabulary: jobs (dentist, doctor, driver, gardener, teacher); suffix -less (toothless, hopeless, helpless); 'th' digraph (thirty, three, throw, tooth); 'wh' digraph (when, what); word families (try, tried; talk, talked, talking, talks; tell, telling, tells, told).
Literary elements: riddle; joke; word play (tooth hurty/two thirty).

Trace and finish the pattern.

Write the date.

Use t to finish these words. Trace the words.

alk alks alked alking

ell ells old elling

Trace then write.

What time is it when

you go to the dentist?

Tooth hurty.

Self-assessment

How many t's are on these two pages?

Draw a star around your best t or T.

Write the date.

Trace.

leopard loafing lazily

Trace then write.

Trace then write.

leap lug lie lift loosen lose

Handwriting: i family letter; head and body letter (ascender) (l).
Grammar: nouns; action verbs (leap, lug, lift); how adverb (lazily); question; question word (Why?); adjectives (big, wrinkly).
Punctuation: full stop; question mark; capital letter to start a sentence.

Spelling and vocabulary: apostrophe for contraction (they're); changing y to i to add -ed or -ly (cried, happily, lazily, messily, tried); elephant, leap, leopard, lie, lift, loosen, lose, lug, wrinkly; homophones (too/to/two); word families (loaf, loafed, loafing, loafs).
Literary elements: joke.

Trace and finish the pattern.

Write the date.

Use l to finish these words. Trace the words.

oaf oafs oafed oafing

Trace then write.

Why are elephants so

wrinkly? They're too big to

fit on the ironing board.

Self-assessment

Are your l's sloping evenly?

Handwriting: i family letter; body and tail letter (descender) (j).
Grammar: nouns; action verbs (jiggle, jostle, jump, juggle); how adverb (jauntily); statement.
Punctuation: full stop; capital letter to start a sentence.

Spelling and vocabulary: jauntily, jester, jog, join, journey, jump; 'le' ending (jiggle, jostle, juggle, single); 'th' digraph (thousand, with); word families (juggle, juggled, juggles, juggling).
Literary elements: Chinese proverb.

Trace and finish the pattern.

Write the date.

Find and trace the body and tail letters.

j h m p n q p g s c j t

Use j to finish these words. Trace the words.

uggle uggles uggled

Trace then write.

The journey of a thousand

miles starts with a single

step.

Self-assessment

How many j's did you write on these two pages?

Circle your best j and J.

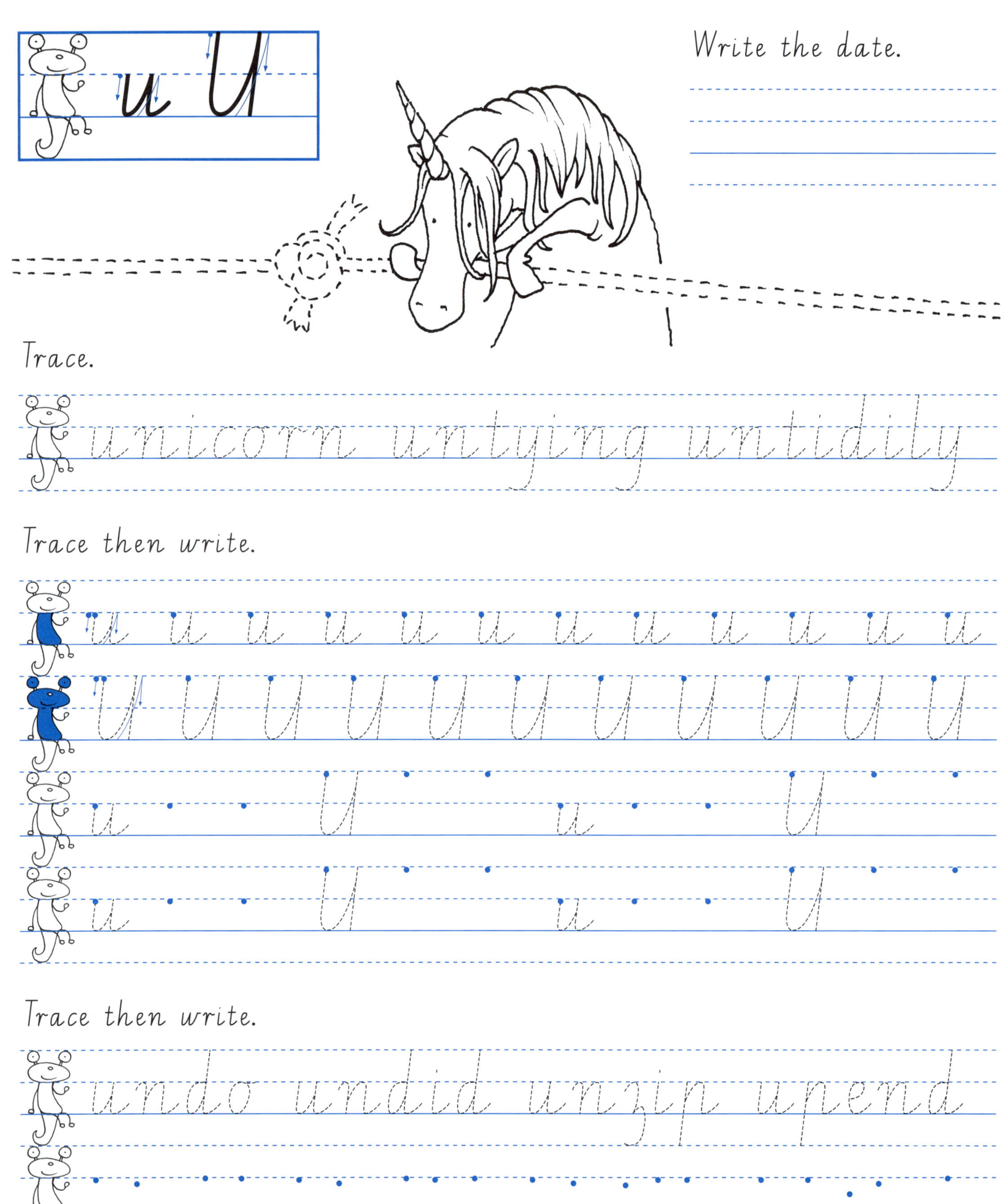

Handwriting: u family letter; body letter (u).
Grammar: nouns; action verbs; how adverbs; antonyms (did/undid); question; question word (What?).
Punctuation: question mark; capital letter to start a sentence.
Spelling and vocabulary: prefix un- (undid, undo, untidily, untying, unzip); suffixes -ing, -ily (untying, untidily); word families (untie, untied, unties, untying); umbrella, under, unicorn, upend.
Literary elements: riddle; joke; homophone word play (rain/rein).

Trace and finish the pattern.

Write the date.

Find and trace u and U.

u v W U n m V u U e U a o u u N

Use u to finish these words. Trace the words.

ntie ntied nties ntying

Trace then write.

What animal needs to

stand under an umbrella?

A reindeer.

Self-assessment

How many u's have you written on this page?

Circle your best u.

y Y

Write the date.

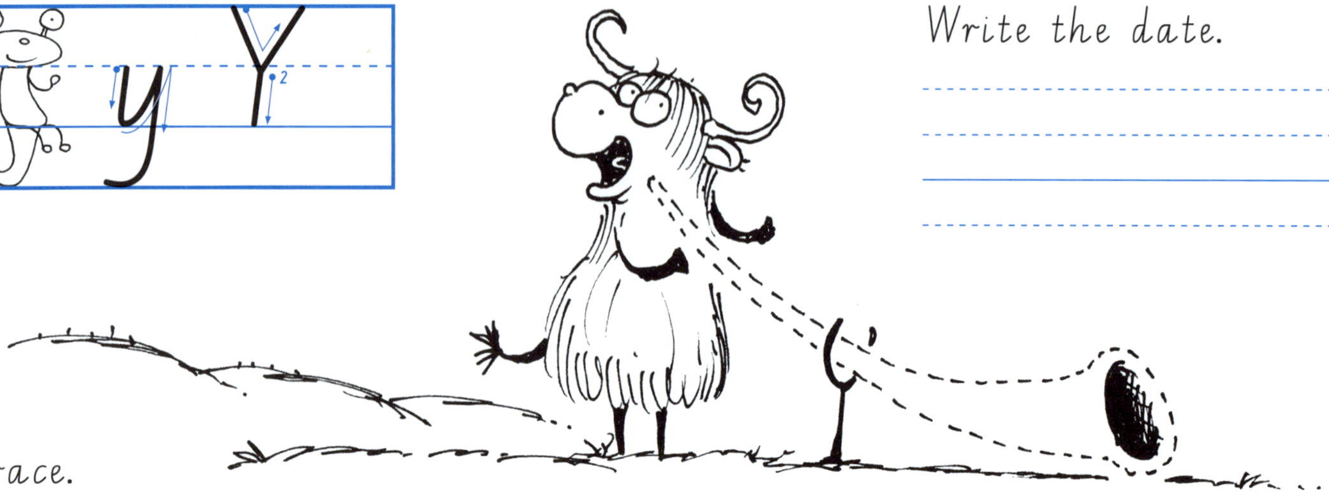

Trace.

yak yodelling yappily

Trace then write.

y y y y y y y y y y y y y y y

Y Y Y Y Y Y Y Y Y Y Y Y

y Y y Y

y Y y Y

Trace then write.

yell yawn cry try yelled yap

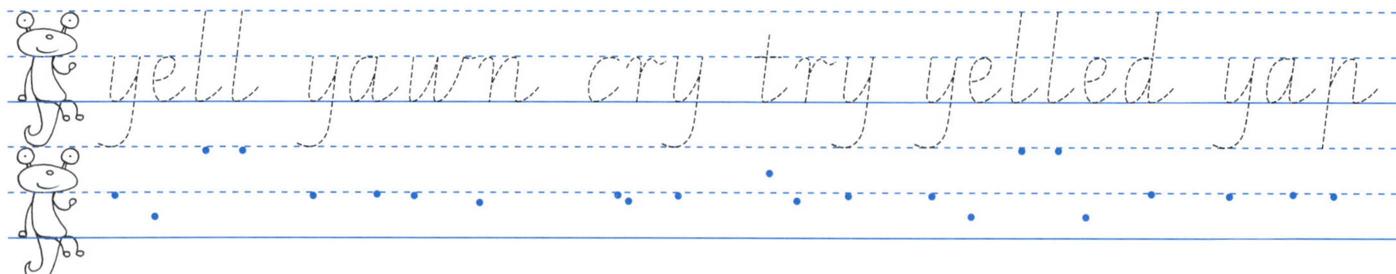

Handwriting: u family letter; body and tail letter (descender) (y).
Grammar: nouns; saying verbs (yell, yelled, cry, yodelling); how adverb (yappily); tense (yell/yelled); question; question word (Where?).
Punctuation: full stop; question mark; capital letter to start a sentence.
Spelling and vocabulary: barking, parking, try, cry, yak, yappily, yawn, yelled; suffixes -ing, -ily, -ed (barking, yappily, yelled); word families (yodel, yodelled, yodelling, yodels).
Literary elements: rhyme (cry/try, barking/parking); riddle; joke; word play (barking/parking).

Trace and finish the pattern.

Write the date.

Use y to finish these words. Trace the words.

odel odels odelled

Trace then write.

Where can you leave your

dog while you shop?

In the barking lot.

Circle the y with the best tail on these two pages.

Underline the y's that could be improved.

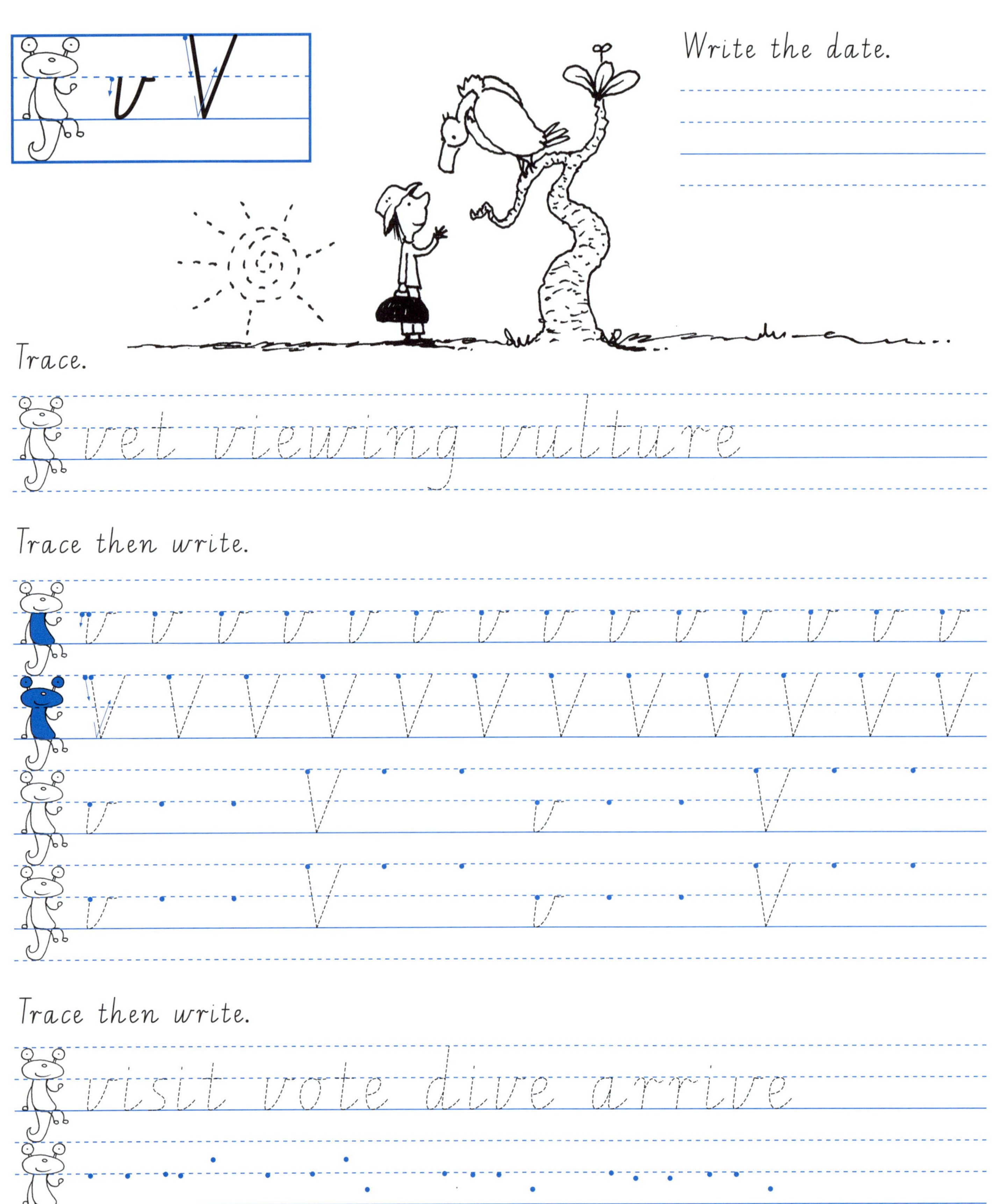

Handwriting: u family letter; body letter (v).
Grammar: nouns; action verbs (viewing, visit, vote, dive, arrive); statement.
Punctuation: full stop; capital letter to start a sentence.

Spelling and vocabulary: arrive, dive, brave, grave, save, behave, vet, viewing, visit, vote, vulture; word families (view, viewed, viewing, views); rhyme (arrive/dive/drive/survive, behave/brave/gave/save).
Literary elements: Aesop (Greek) fable 'The Four Oxen and the Lion', moral: United we stand divided we fall.

Trace and finish the pattern.

Write the date.

Write.

v v

Use v to finish these words. Trace the words.

sa_e bra_e ga_e beha_e

_iew _iews _iewed _iewing

Trace then write.

United we stand,

divided we fall.

Self-assessment

Are all of your v's the same size?

Handwriting: u family letter; body letter (w).
Grammar: proper noun (Wendy); thinking verbs (wanted, wished); how adverb (wildly); past tense (waved, wished); question; question word (Why?).
Punctuation: question mark; capital letter to start a sentence.
Spelling and vocabulary: 'ow' (throw, wallowing, window); 'a' for short 'o' sound (wanted, watch, wallow); suffixes -ing, -ly, -ed (wallowing, wildly, wished, waved); word families (wallow, wallowed, wallowing, wallows; want, wanted, wants).
Literary elements: riddle; joke; homonym word play (wrist watch/watch time fly).

Trace and finish the patterns.

Write the date.

Use w to finish these words. Trace the words.

allo allo s allo ed

ant ants anted

Trace then write.

Why did Wendy throw her

watch out the window?

To see time fly.

Self-assessment

Draw a square around the word that is your best handwriting on each page.

Handwriting: u family letter; head and body letter (ascender) (b).
Grammar: proper noun (Bob); saying verbs (buzzed, burped); how adverb (badly); question; question word (Why?).
Punctuation: full stop; question mark; capital letter to start a sentence.

Spelling and vocabulary: badly, battery, beagle, because, bump, bury, buzzed; 'ur' vowel digraph (burped, burn); word families (behave, behaved, behaves, behaving; burp, burped, burping, burps).
Literary elements: riddle; joke; word play (died); onomatopoeia (buzz, burped).

Trace and finish the pattern.

Write the date.

Use b to finish these words. Trace the words.

ehave ehaves ehaved

urp urps urped urping

Trace then write.

Why did Bob bury his

torch? Because the battery

died.

Self-assessment

Draw a frame around your best B on these two pages.

Trace then write.

Write the date.

0 1 2

3 4 5 6 7

8 9 10 11 12

13 14 15 16

17 18 19 20

There are 7 days in a week

and 12 months in a year.

Trace.

There are 365 days in a year

and 366 days in a leap year.

Self-assessment

Draw a star around your best numeral.

Draw a triangle around a numeral you could improve.

Trace then write.

Write the date.

30 days has

September, April, June and

November. All the rest

have 31 except February

which has 28 days clear

and 29 each leap year.

Self-assessment Draw a frame around each numeral.

Tick the numeral with the highest value.

How many words name months of the year? ☐

Write the date.

Trace then write.

10 ten 20 twenty 30 thirty

40 forty 50 fifty 60 sixty

70 seventy 80 eighty

90 ninety 100 one hundred

1st first 2nd second 3rd third

Self-assessment

Circle and label your BEST handwriting on this page as 1st, 2nd or 3rd.

Trace then write in correct NUMBER order.

fifty sixty forty

Write the date.

Trace then link the numeral to the number word.

thirty 8 eighty 9 90 seventy

70 nine 80 eight 30 ninety

Trace then write in correct ALPHABETICAL order.

twelve fifteen eleven

Trace then write in correct ALPHABETICAL order.

twenty eighteen nineteen

Trace then write in correct ALPHABETICAL order.

fourteen twelve seventeen ten

Self-assessment

Draw a box around your neatest handwritten word.

Draw a circle around your best handwritten numeral.

Trace then write.

Write the date.

Knock, knock.

Who's there?

Who.

Who who?

I didn't know

you were an owl!

Remember to make your letters a consistent size.

Self-assessment

Circle your neatest words.

Write the date.

Trace then write. Link each joke to its answer.

What kind of key lives in a forest?

magpie
mutt-erial
monkey

What are clothes for a dog made from?

What pie can fly?

Are your letters all the same size?   

Copy the jokes in your best handwriting.

Write the date.

Who has a face, two hands and ticks? A teacher.

Why did the Cyclops close her school? She only had one pupil.

Self-assessment

Is your writing easy for others to read?   

Remember correct pencil hold. The index finger pulls towards your body. The thumb pushes away.

Write the date.

Trace then write.

aA bB cC dD eE

fF gG hH iI jJ kK

lL mM nN oO pP

qQ rR sS tT uU

vV wW xX yY zZ

Self-assessment

Is your pencil grip comfortable?

Write the date.

ant beagle camel deer elephant fish gorilla hippo ibis jaguar kangaroo leopard meerkat numbat owl peacock quokka rat snake turtle unicorn vulture walrus fox yak zonkey

Copy the alphabetical list of animals.

Does your writing hand and arm move freely?

Progressive assessments

Each term, write the sentence.
Colour the stars to rate your handwriting.
See how your handwriting improves!

The quick brown fox jumps over the lazy dog.

Term 1 Date ____________

Rating ☆ ☆ ☆ ☆ ☆

Term 2 Date ____________

Rating ☆ ☆ ☆ ☆ ☆

Progressive assessments continued

The quick brown fox jumps over the lazy dog.

Term 3 Date ______________

Rating ☆ ☆ ☆ ☆ ☆

Term 4 Date ______________

Rating ☆ ☆ ☆ ☆ ☆